Charles L. Peterson

OF TIME AND PLACE

THE
WHITE
DOOR
PUBLISHING CO.

Charles L. Peterson

OF TIME AND PLACE

Charles L. Peterson

Copyright ©1994. The White Door Publishing Company, Inc.
All art is copyrighted and reproduced with the permission of C.L. Peterson, Inc.
All Rights Reserved.

Editors:
Mark E. Quale
Susan Peterson

Design:
Bill Lundborg

Essay:
Norbert Blei

Photography:
Pat Goetzinger pp. 2, 7, 9, 10, 11, 12, 13, 14, 17, 19
Susan Hass p. 18
Mark Gubin p. 8

Printed and bound in the United States of America
by Watt/Peterson, Inc.

ISBN 0-9643438-0-0
Hard Cover "Gallery" Edition
Single Edition of 2,500, 1994

ISBN 0-9643438-1-9
Soft Cover Edition,
First Printing, 1994; Second Printing, 1997

Library of Congress Catalog Card Number:
94-61429

Published by:
The White Door Publishing Company, Inc.
Post Office Box 427
New London, MN 56273
(320) 796-2209

We are very pleased to introduce you to the art of one of America's great artists, Charles L. Peterson. While any presentation of selected works falls short in representing a lifetime of painting, we hope it does serve as a valid introduction.

Our intent has been to allow you to view the work in much the same way you would as you walk through a museum exhibit. Each painting stands alone, uncluttered, without distraction or direction, for each to do with as they choose. Near some of the paintings you notice a small display containing a clipping from the artist's sketchbook, clearly in rough form, but shedding light on the creative process. As you walk the room you hear the artist's own words, not as narration; simply a collage of comments regarding his art, his philosophy, his life.

As you go through the exhibit many of the individual stops may leave you wanting to know more. Our hope is, however, that by the time you complete it you will feel you have gotten to know a little better this extraordinary artist . . . and that you will look forward to taking the tour again and again.

Mark E. Quale, President
The White Door Publishing Company, Inc.

TABLE OF CONTENTS

7

CHARLES L. PETERSON – THE MAN

The Presence of the Past by Norbert Blei   9

21

CHARLES L. PETERSON – THE WORK

93

CHARLES L. PETERSON – LISTING OF WORKS AND BIOGRAPHY

DEDICATION

To Mother: whose genetic gift gave me the facility to become a painter and the courage to face the challenge of it; to Dad, without whose patience I could not have endured it; to elder brothers Bob and Dick who expected me to try; and to my extended family who gave me their love and encouragement.

To my wife Susan and our three daughters, their husbands, and their sons, each of whom in their various ways, offer forthright responses to my work, helping me to keep in mind my obligation to my art and my patrons. By their easy forebearance, they make possible my devotion to my work.

To the numerous associates who have been critically supportive throughout my career; Museum and gallery directors, publishers, editors and art directors, colleagues and fellow professionals, and the many, many friends whose interest have helped shape my work.

And finally, to the patrons who have supported my painting over the course of a lifetime and, more recently, the collectors of my reproductions, all of whom together make it possible for me to live and work in this beautiful place. Their enthusiasm renews my determination to become the best painter I am capable of being.

THE MAN

CHARLES L. PETERSON: THE PRESENCE OF THE PAST

BY NORBERT BLEI

There is a comfort and truth in the familiar: the hands and faces of the old; a family reunion outside a white farm house in spring; a village in winter; a country church; a concert in the park; men at work in the fields and at sea. To return to that which lends beauty and meaning to our lives, where memory comes upon us like a prayer. *Yes, that is the way it was, we tell ourselves. The way it should be. Where I belong.*

There is a need to hold the time and image, for whatever reason. Travelers and artists know this in their bones. We are always journeying back in time, in search of where we find ourselves today.

The paintings of Charles L. Peterson call us home. Haunt our attention. Celebrate the strength and dignity of man at work. At peace within himself . . . in communion with others in time and place. A world familiar and compelling, where every detail of the image whispers: *Do not forget.*

"It's true," he will tell you, "my life has centered on that theme, memory. The things that I paint . . . I think probably there's a natural tendency in all of us to reflect on our own past. I think it's a positive contribution to our time to remind it of some of the values of the past which are worthwhile."

For tourist and resident alike, driving north down Highway 42 on Wisconsin's Door Peninsula toward Ephraim, winding through fields and orchards, panoramic views of bluffs and bays, suggests a landscape bordering on the serene. A double image: what you see and what you think you see. Approaching Peninsula State Park, descending in a gentle glide down the hill into the village itself . . . the blue waters of Eagle Harbor ahead, the road gently turning till suddenly the village of Ephraim ("doubly fruitful") opens in white buildings along the shore, trailing up the hillside, evoking memories of the distant past in the visible present.

The immediacy of the authentic. The illusion of art.

Whatever the season: winter – the painter, Charles "Chick" Peterson, at peace, in place, quietly at work in his studio within the white-on-white village, envisioning a watercolor, *Jule Tiden* perhaps, with Anderson's Dock covered in snow, moonlight spilling over the bluff and still harbor, the artist arranging the composition, his relationship – and ours – to what he sees. Whatever the time: day or night – the lights of the village reflecting over the night waters of the bay, the glow of the white church steeples. Whatever the color of the harbor or sky in each season: the artist softening his palette, working the Prussian Blue to a hue some admirers have come to call "Peterson blue," Ephraim hovers like a specter above and along the water's edge. Time past and time present, indeed. The artist conjuring his own vision: look and see. Now look again. And truly see.

Ephraim: a place called home, "doubly fruitful," for Charles Peterson. A setting worthy of the painter who comfortably inhabits it, as it inhabits him, nourishing, protecting his local identity, while at the same time extending his artistry and reputation far beyond the village.

His personal history on this stark and shining peninsula shaped by the Niagara escarpment is not that of the native of Scandinavian ancestry who pioneered this place, but of the outsider of Scandinavian blood with a scholarly regard for the past, and a profound reverence for the native working people from pioneer times to the present – farmers, fishermen, seamen, early loggers.

His introduction to the county came as a young man. "I was thrilled by this area. I came to Door County from Illinois for the first time right after World War II with a friend, Del Neil, and we camped in Peninsula Park. 1947, I believe. I climbed the lookout tower, went up to Gills Rock and saw an eagle. It was wonderful, the cliffs and the trees, the air, and the water. We both loved sailing and the lake was enormously impressive. We thought we had come to heaven."

Twenty years later he would return for good. And explore the area from another dimension entirely: an artist in search of his subject . . . in perfecting his artistry.

"It wasn't until I graduated from high school, mid-year, that I studied art. I wasn't going to be eighteen till April and I didn't face the draft for

several months. So I took a post-graduate high school course in art. My mother went to the teacher, Claudia Abel, and said, 'My son is interested in art, but he won't take a high school class because he doesn't want to do the things that kids do in high school class.' And old Claudia, who was a tough old girl, said: 'You tell that boy to get in here and he can draw anything he wants.' And so I did."

His term of service in the Navy was brief, as he jokingly recalls: "I was only in about a year, fifteen months. I got to the Pacific, but when the Japanese heard I was coming, they quit."

Returning home to Elgin, Illinois, he began work as an apprentice artist in a religious publishing company in his hometown. And from there was hired by the prestigious Leo Burnett advertising agency in Chicago, where he stayed for six months while waiting to get into commercial art school to seriously pursue a profession as illustrator.

"By the time I went to art school I had been strongly impressed by Dohanos, Fawcett, and N.C. Weyth. Rockwell through the Saturday Evening Post. It was in our house and I was inspired by that. There's nothing inherent in illustration that prevents it being great art. N.C. Wyeth was enormously exciting to me as a kid. His wonderful books for boys. I thought that was what I wanted to be, an illustrator."

Ironically, it was while studying commercial art for two years at the American Academy in Chicago, at the age of twenty, that he had the opportunity to experience serious art for the first time.

"I would spend the noon hour gobbling a sandwich and then going to the Art Institute. That was a wonderful education. I remember Hopper's *Nighthawk*. Hopper struck me very early in art school. He was an inspiration. I love the power of his simple realism. Andrew Wyeth became a much later influence. A kind of confirmation in that I was moving his way. I think Wyeth imparts dignity if not a nobility to common objects by his excruciating scrutiny."

He entered Marietta College in Ohio in 1951. "I was disillusioned with what I was doing and where I was going in commercial art. Just at that moment an old high school friend, Ray Barnhart, came through and urged me to go to college. 'Take liberal arts,' he said. 'Expand your horizons.' And I did."

"The whole commercial art school experience was good. It's sympathetic with my personality. I believe in the traditional values of representation. It's certainly not the only basis for art but it is valid. That was excellent training. The commercial art application, however, was not a good exprience for me. By chance and by lack of saleable skill, I didn't see I was going to get into what I imagined would be a satisfying career. Specifically, I suppose, I didn't see that I was going to become a Saturday Evening Post cover artist.

"That was disillusioning, or maybe, that was an awakening. And then . . . I loved college. I loved the intellectual experience of academic life. And also, because I was older and living with a faculty family, I was exposed to faculty life, which I greatly enjoyed. So I saw that would be a good career."

For fourteen years he pursued the best of both worlds: the academic life, where he accepted a fulltime position as a professor of art at Marietta College in 1959, and the first real stirrings of life as a struggling artist in Door County, where his inlaws had a summerhome next to Anderson's Dock, and where he spent summers painting.

"Right away I began sketching at Anderson's Dock – boats, people, the regattas. One of those came back to me this year. A painting I did before I moved here. A little watercolor sketch of a regatta of the Seagull fleet at Ephraim. The owner had it on his boat for twenty years or so. The painting was completely ruined because it had been in sunlight too much, and it was done with student paints. He sent it back because he thought I would be amused. And I was. I turned it over and on the back I had written a price: ten dollars.

"There are still some paintings in the family done in that period when I sold them right from the dock. The prices were in the fifty to the hundred dollar range then. I was teaching, of course, and this was just pure vacation, but it began to make me conscious of the fact that it might be possible to seriously sell work here."

In 1973, at the age of 46, he left the security of a tenured professorship at Marietta College and moved to Ephraim with his wife, Susan, and their three daughters, Eve 14, Beth 13, and Sara 8, to pursue a life as a serious American artist.

The studio of Charles Peterson is a study of the man himself. Peaceful,

bright, secluded (behind the village), orderly, expansive, private but welcoming. A part of, yet apart from, the home. Traditional yet modern. A highly varnished wooden floor reflects a rosy warmth upon the white walls and ceiling, filling the room with a sense of reverence for thought and work. A sign above the door reads:

Thou, O Lord, dost sell us all good things at the price of labor.
— Leonardo DaVinci

Aside from a radio kept tuned to classical music on the public station, there is no sound, few distractions. The walls are mostly bare. There is a Manet etching – a portrait of Baudelaire. A few of his own paintings, past and present, hang on the east wall for the artist's own observation. His drawing table, easel, work table, occupy a relatively small island of quiet activity and contemplation beneath a north wall of double windows and beautiful light which streams over the man and his work as he faces east. The same north windows where he might occasionally look out upon his house, a flower garden, cedar woods, road, and in the distance, toward the northwest, sky, bluff, and water – the essential trademarks of the county. Light and inspiration at the artist's beckon.

A set of low bookshelves along the west and north wall hold cameras, photographs for study, and reference works reflective of Peterson's dedication to detail and authenticity. *National Geographic* magazines: 1966 to the present; two sets of Time-Life books: *The Seafarers,* and *The West*; a 1902 Sears and Roebuck catalog; Civil War books; reference works on schooners and yachts; collections of *Wooden Boat* and *Sail* magazines; a few modern art books; and a virtual treasure of the artist's own sketchbooks – beautiful, precise, though mere working pencil and ink sketches to later develop into full-blown paintings – from 1975 to the present.

Also on the west wall, his back to it as he paints, almost unnoticeable: a mirror. The double image once again. The artist oblivious of its presence. But for those instances when the work demands he turn, look back at the reflection, catch something of himself for reference. Verify a gesture of a human image: an arm outstretched, a hand grasping a farm implement, a visage of endurance. Real. Honest. Exact.

As real, honest and exact as the artist himself. A quiet, gentle dignity to his presence. Tall, lean, almost always casually dressed. An impeccably neat painter. White hair, white beard, glasses. The bearing and certainty of a college professor in discussion. A sharp wit in conversation. A born storyteller. A man as alive in the world of the intellect as the world of every day life. Thankful. Contented with who he is, where he lives, what he does.

"I love this studio. When you describe this job to people who don't know what the creative process is, they're kind of disappointed. It sounds like an ordinary work-a-day job. And that's what it is! They think that writing or composing or painting is a joy. And it's not. It's an eternal challenge, thank God. At least so far. I think it's a privilege to be able to work in this way, but it's not a happy life. It's a frustrating life. You always fall short of the possibilities of the problem. And yet, there is the dreamer in me . . . and I suppose it's fundamental to anyone who continues in the creative field. That it is possible to come closer."

A typical day for him in the studio begins around 8:30. "Any creative decision should be made early. I'm a morning man."

After more than three hours of painting (or problem solving, as he often refers to it) he breaks for lunch around noon ("I'm within two minutes of the dining table.") and returns to his studio again for a full afternoon's work.

"In winter, in the depths of December, January, when the sun fails at 3:30 I quit then. And in summer it goes much longer. In summer I taper off around 4:30 or 5 o'clock. Under pressure I'll work evenings, but I don't like working that way and that, in part, is due to my addiction to this north window. I hate to paint under artificial light.

"The typical painting nowadays has gotten very complex so it's likely to spread over a long time. When I finished art school, three hours was normal for a watercolor. I'm now at three weeks on some of these complicated ones."

On his drawing board is a sketch of a farmer outside an open barn door, one arm bent forward, the hand clutching the handle of a pitchfork, the other arm angled against his body. His facial expression . . . difficult to fathom at this stage.

The artist consults his black sketch book for the preliminary stages of the drawing.

"It developed very quickly. I had a feeling for doing a working man, that's all, and it became a farmer without any effort. And that suggested a vertical composition. A standing man. I wanted a limited background. It just became a barn door. I started sketching just to make shape."

Not every painting flows smoothly from the original conception in the sketch book, to the complete drawing, to the fully realized watercolor. The artist admits his struggles with *Country Doctor* as he views a number of false starts on the painting. Struggles which confirm the diligence and dedication of Charles Peterson.

"I actually did eight starts on *Country Doctor.* And each of those represents approximately a day. That's part of the perversity of what I'm talking about, using watercolor for this kind of subject. But that's another part of my personality: I persist. I think: *If only I try harder it will be alright.*

"Some nights when I leave the studio I feel pretty good. Sometimes I bring the painting in the house with me. Put it on the hearth. Look at it in lamplight. That'll be one way it's judged – living with the painting. I often make notes as I look at it, things that occur to me then that I ought to consider.

"So, roughly, I probably spend six to eight days of painting on a typical complex painting . . . of actual painting, distinguished from the development of sketches. Leonardo kept the Mona Lisa with him all of his life for a variety of reasons, among them the fact he never considered it finished."

As far as the artist's own palette: "I have simply reduced mine from the impressionist palette which was my training. I've gone to extremes now. I'm down to three colors: Prussian Blue, Yellow Ocher, and Cadmium Red Medium. Whatever the colors in my work, they tend toward neutralized colors or grayed colors. When I look at my paintings in comparison to the broad field of painting in general, they tend toward the grayer, softer colors instinctively."

In total command of his talents at this stage in his artistic career, and without a hint of arrogance, Peterson quietly admits, "I know I can paint almost anything. I'm a master of the techniques I use. I haven't painted an angel because I've never seen one. But if you'll show me one, I'll paint it."

He rejects the notion of "Peterson Blue," a color often associated with his work. "No. I rely on Prussian Blue and I think I'm using it quite flexibly because my normal color range is grayed . . . it's a Swedish thing," he laughs, "neutralized colors. I'm not dealing in intense colors. An impressionist would need a lot of bright colors. He puts them side by side and from a distance they merge . . . beautiful. I like the desert. I'm convinced it was designed by a Swede. Except after the rain, when the flowers come out."

To watch Peterson paint is to witness magic in the making. Illusion and reality. Paper, paint, brush, and water. Beauty evolving from mere brush strokes. The tension between eye and hand. To hear Peterson's voice engaged in describing the actual process, is to eavesdrop on a master's class in painting.

Moistening the palette with a brush, he studies again his painting of *The Farmer*, applying color to the barn where the figure of the farmer is standing.

"It's just a wash on a wet surface but it's got some interesting settlement going on. Some of the pigments will float to the top and create some really beautiful textures spontaneously. Now it's only a preliminary wash and it's going to get a heck of a lot darker eventually. I'm not sure yet about streaks of light between the barn boards, but I might put in a few now while I'm at it.

"It's a common theme: ordinary people engaged in ordinary activities. But this guy is having a thought. There, now . . . that's drying up. I'm going to try a warm wash merging to very dark at the top, just to begin what's going on inside the barn. It's going to be warm, yellowish down here because I think hay, so I'll start this way . . . I'm going to stop here because the threshold is going to have a board nailed inside. This is a door within a door. Now I'm going to add blue to this and I'll get that very dark neutral which will serve for the shadow, distant part of the barn and begin to produce some depth in there. It's a little bit intense, blue, so I'm going to add some neutralizing red to it immediately. Now it looks warm, and so we're somewhere in between and we'll just have to let it dry to see what it does.

"Because I can run an additional wash over whatever is necessary. I'm going to drag this down to begin to darken the stuff that's in the barn and let it merge. Only preliminary. I'm confident I'll be painting over this several times before I'm done. I intend sunlight shining on this, casting a shadow. And then I intend a very dark shadow back here. I see now that I have altered the composition considerably from what I have here, for better or worse. At the moment, I'm not prepared to judge because all of this stuff confuses my concept of what the composition is going to be.

"This is going to be a worn out pair of overalls, so I'm going to paint them with worn, highlight areas, lighter blue . . . that kind of stuff, and a conventional chambray workshirt. Just an ordinary farmer. I had sketched stone here, and I see that I was thinking stone there, but I believe I'll do the whole thing as a wooden barn. It could go either way. There . . . that's nice. It looks like porous wood. It's fairly dry up there. Dramatic. So it's a matter of inventing something to produce a texture you can use. It doesn't look anything like hay now but it has a manure pile look to it at least. Kind of a nice settling on the pigment there. Those are qualities that are accidental. You understand what a paper will do, so you set up the conditions and then hope for the best. I'll take this a little further this afternoon."

All of the reproductions in The Memories Collection reflect Peterson's fascination with what he calls the 'ghost image,' a technique and a theme which both confirm and heighten his concern for the past. Gives his work yet another perspective. A sense of layers, as if one were peeling things back to an original source or turning back the pages of a calendar.

Peterson jokingly tells of a complaint his publisher received one time concerning the ghost image in his paintings. "You're pulling a fast one," the complainant said. He was convinced that the artist was doing two different paintings and super imposing them by double exposure because "this can't be done in watercolor."

"My response was, it shouldn't be done in watercolor," says Peterson, "but it obviously can be if you're perverse enough. It's an inappropriate use of the medium. And yet, I don't want to be unfair to myself. I think it's inappropriate for the conventional view of watercolor as a transparent, spontaneous medium. Obviously, I'm using it in a controlled way, but I think that is consistent with my personality. I think it's an honest use for me.

"I believe it carries a legitimate message. More than that, I believe it carries a legitimate challenge to a viewer in terms of pure abstraction because the composition is quite complex. It requires a lot of looking to organize it, in two different ways. One is the landscape and the other is what the figures do to the sense of balance."

His wife, Sue, feels that the origin of his ghost image paintings can be found in a painting called *Memory,* which he painted in 1975. It was a painting of a shipwrecked Great Lakes schooner on a sandy shore with a spirit of the captain hovering over it.

"But, in fact, my thinking is that the ideas for it go much farther back than that," claims the artist. "In graduate school I made a conscientious study of the development of cubism. And Picasso's simultaneity shows us interpenetration of objects and their background. So, that idea of seeing through an object and, most importantly, I think, doing it as a compositional device was important in my thinking."

Yet the artist concedes that the technique goes back even further, as far back as the Renaissance and the use of representational techniques involved with spiritual experience . . . Velazquez, El Greco.

"So, basically, realistic technique applied to a spiritual experience became a part of my awareness. I think my development of the ghost image came from those two general directions. The formal idea of cubism, essentially an abstraction and therefore a compositional force, invaded my awareness and I think that's what it amounts to now: the ghost image. It offers an enriched composition because it's a double composition of which the second part is quite subtle. You shift in midstream."

Known for being somewhat of a reserved person, rather self-effacing for an artist, it comes a surprise to discover that Peterson is more personally involved in his paintings than most people would imagine, especially in

The Memories Collection where the ghost images often reflect the artist's own past.

"I appear frequently in the series. *The Family Reunion* has the personalities of my family in it. My grandmother, in the foreground, is real and my Aunt Angeline, spoon in hand, sticking her head out of the kitchen. She was always in charge of any cooking going on. Uncle Harold, a superintendent of schools, and his daughter, Carol Ann. There's my grandfather. I am this creature here, and there's my cousin Billy. We just spotted each other and we're going to start racing. My Aunt Eva. My two brothers, Dick and Bob. Aunt Helen. But they're loose drawings showing, I think, the varieties of family personalities which would be detectable in any family. I think it's a universal theme. A message for us all, I believe.

"I think that *Family Reunion* stems from a nostalgia for that family. My dad's family was typically remote, even though most of them lived right in Elgin, Illinois. But mother's family was very close, very warm. I'm literally in *The Concert* as well. My mother and dad are on the bench over on the right side. And I'm asleep beside mother, and my brother is leaning over from the bench behind. In *Evening Lemonade* I'm asleep on my Aunt Angeline's lap. It's our porch . . . and that's Esther Splitgerber sitting alone next door. Frank has died. Yes, yes . . . very personal.

"I've done self-portraits. But in another way, too, I appear in all of them,

I'm sure, and that's in the autobiographical idea that I think is inherent in any artist's style: he paints what he knows."

As for his masterful marine paintings, noted for their authentic detail of ships and sailing conditions, his own relationship to water as a theme, a way of life reflected in his art: "I suppose that's personal. I love sailing. It satisfies something in my needs, my soul. It's a fluid and graceful kind of action.

"The pleasure in sailing and the observation of sailing is fundamental to effective marine painting, I think, because one ought to understand the forces at work. That's obvious. My own preference for 'work' as a subject. Working man. Working sails.

"Boats that are used for work. It's a collaboration between man and his invention and nature that appeals to me. In that sense, it's akin to any working theme. The farmer is no different from the sailor. He has to understand the forces at work in his world and make use of them. And that's exactly what my experience is in sailing. I have to try and understand what the wind is doing with reference to the water, and my handling of the boat has to take those things into account. Otherwise, I've failed."

His work, at this stage in his career, falls into three areas: his own private art, painting for reproductions, and painting for commission.

"Many artists hate commission painting. It doesn't particularly bother me. It's a satisfying thing. I don't accept something that doesn't interest me. I do them as I can or as I feel ready for them. Most of them are open-ended, and I accept only those that I think I can do justice to.

"A great anything – a piece of music or a book – can result from any subject. The subject is assigned, or it's acquired some way by the creative person. It isn't the subject that determines the greatness of the final result. It's what the artist does with the subject. Almost the whole length of art history has been commissioned art work. I think of myself from that tradition. Michelangelo didn't do the Sistine Chapel on speculation."

Art needs no explanation. No defense. Only one critic matters: the artist himself. Beyond that? Most serious artists desire some recognition and understanding. The voyage is marked by self-discovery, the continual pursuit of excellence, criticism, and a modicum of self-doubt. Charles Peterson is no exception.

"I try to arouse an honest emotion and avoid sentiment or sentimentality. Self-doubt enters at times. But I've come to the position that my work is valid in that I'm trying to remind my time that there are worthwhile qualities from the past, having to do with work and family and religion, the spiritual experience, and those things are worth remembering. In fact, I think those things are important to our time because we are losing our structure as a society. I believe that's what I'm painting. And if that's nostalgia, then I'm nostalgic."

Ephraim centers much of Peterson's art and life, past and present, though his work and reputation have grown far beyond this small village on the Door Peninsula.

"Winter here is wonderful for me to work. There is no distraction. If there are more than six cars a day on our road, it's a source of alarm. I just love the sustained period of no interruption. I paint the year around, but I may be a better painter in winter. I sense an upcoming period of real involvement in my art after New Years. That's very nice. I've got a long time. No rush. I like to paint winter. Everything is quite clear.

"I live a very quiet life. I love having a silent community of creative people living here. It's important to me that they are out there. But I don't need to see them every day."

Within the village, within this Midwestern landscape, it's not a question of if Charles Peterson will be remembered or how, given the extensive body of his work, the masterful compositions where he held time still, held everything in beauty, balance, and harmony forever. It's a only a question of how the artist himself would like to be remembered.

"Degas wrote his own epitaph: *He loved to draw.* I wouldn't mind being remembered that way."

THE WORK

*I treasure the silence here, the hushed quiet of our winters.
You can hear a pileated woodpecker a half-mile away.
I feel at peace in Ephraim.*

Morning is clearly my best time.
Who knows where the ideas
come from; it may be literature,
something I have read or it might
come from a mood generated
by some music I heard at breakfast
– and I will start sketching . . .

Mine is an adventurous, storytelling kind of art.

*H*aving visited Anderson's store (now a museum) many times I imagined it through the eyes of a young boy, myself perhaps, wistfully gazing at all the shiny gadgets, jackknives, the tempting display of gumballs and hard candies, listening to the friendly chatter of neighbors, and smelling the freshly ground coffee. Adolf Anderson, the shy, hard-working proprietor is silently looking on from the hardware department.

*S*unday Hitch, *The Stall*
and *Recitation* are characteristic of a group
of paintings I have done that intertwine
a solid, realistic image with a translucent,
"ghostly" one. Many of these have been
reproduced and are known as "The
Memories Collection." These paintings
are like a layered puzzle. First you see the
tractor, school desk, old tugboat, whatever
it is. Then, as I encourage the viewer to
move through the painting – using a road,
or fence or ray of light – he becomes
aware of the spectral figures, the images
of people whose lives once connected with
those places. This awareness produces a
new compositional force; a shifting sense
of balance and interest. Artistically it's a
challenge I enjoy.

Sunday Hitch, 1989

The Stall, 1985

*L*ight defines form. I use light to strengthen the composition, using it to lead the eye into the painting. The effect of light needs to be logical, the way it really is, but we can manipulate the distribution of patterns to encourage the eye to move around. A successful painting will manipulate light to draw you in, to intrigue you, and ultimately (hopefully) evoke some response from you.

I delight in the life of kids. Kids regularly remind us of all the things that make life special . . . like a fine day with fresh snow to give everything a new look, somehow different and exciting.

32

*I'm intrigued by lives and
personalities from the past,
and those things formerly useful
and vital to their lives —
an old piece of machinery
or a boat . . .*

C.L. PETERSON

"And what is the Sea?" asked Will.
"The Sea!" cried the miller,
"Lord help us all,
It is the greatest thing God made!"

ROBERT LOUIS STEVENSON

I find a special appeal in water. I have conciously chosen to live near it – I look out over the harbor from my deck every day. Water is a wonderful challenge in painting because it has an astonishing range of moods, from mirror-like placidity, to truly frightening violence. Once, while sailing, I experienced a true gale with winds gusting up to 58 knots, so I have enormous respect for even a small body of water like Green Bay. The process of expressing the power or the peacefulness of water in my paintings is endlessly challenging.

Rendezvous, 1992

Tartar and Pamir, 1990

*"All that which concerns the sea is profound and final.
The sea provides visions, darknesses, revelations."*

HILAIRE BELLOC

*M*emory is the first painting I did of this style, juxtaposing the spectral human images with historical objects – ravaged by time. I came up with this idea of painting the captain's spirit hovering over his vessel, merely recalling the incident, not mourning. He was a tough, practical man. His body is vaporous, but not as translucent as I paint them now. Over time, the "memories" concept has evolved, but as near as I can remember, this marks the beginning.

I was raised among working class people and continue to have a deep respect for people who make a living by working with their hands. I admire the fishermen who still go out and risk their lives everyday. And the farmers, men and women, clearing rocks out of their fields. It was, and is, a hard but honest way of life. They made what they could of their lives by the constant labor of their own two hands.

*I paint almost anything except sunsets, butterflies
and beautiful women. There's nothing I can do to improve them.
Whereas, an old farmyard might need
some clarification.*

*"Thou O Lord dost sell us
all good things
at the price of labor."*

LEONARDO DAVINCI

*M*any years ago, it would be about 20 now, I wrote that quote by Leonardo DaVinci on a scrap of brown matboard and stuck it up over the door to my studio. It was just a whim, but it hangs up there still. I guess it captures my feelings on the subject of my work, and my life in general.

I prize barns. I think they reflect an organic relationship between man and his efforts to live in nature. A wooden barn! That's a wonderful organic structure. A functional structure. They're disappearing and I regret that.

Though painting is not necessarily a life of pleasure, it is endlessly challenging and fascinating.

When I was a young man it was a fantasy to think of living from one's painting. It seemed like a hopeless dream. Surprisingly, it has become possible for me and I'm very grateful for the support I've had.

As I get older, I'm becoming more fanatical about my work. I'm conscious of my mortality, so I've become quite jealous of my time and energy. It's a basic human urge, I guess, to leave something worthwhile behind and to try and improve in some small way the life we all share. The fact that I am able to indulge my passion for painting, and make a living at it, is truly a privilege.

*I*t's the random chance of two photographs falling on my desk that started the creative process that eventually became *Wood Sorrel and Mud Bay . . .* One was a softly lit image of my grandson Nicholas through a window; the other an old black and white of what Emma Toft fondly referred to as her "fishing shack." I didn't know Emma Toft personally – just that she was a Door County native and was much admired for her dedication to the preservation of North Bay wetlands. She was a free spirit, a naturalist. I like to think that the wood sorrel on the sill is there waiting to be transplanted.

VIOLET W,
SOMETIMES
HOUSE PLANT

YELLOW
IS COMMON

PLEASANT ACID TASTE
WOODSORREL

Sabbath at Sea, 1990 – Pencil

Sabbath at Sea, 1991 – Oil

I don't have any fixed goal except to paint as well as I possibly can. That's enough.

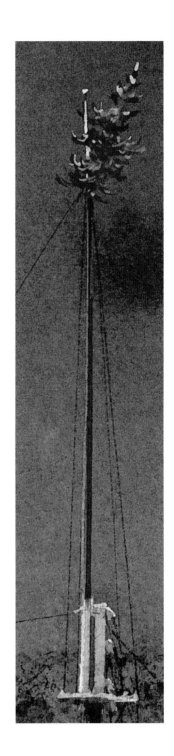

*O*ver the years I think I've drawn and painted Anderson's Dock from every conceivable angle. I suppose I've worked with the bloody thing long enough that I feel at home with it. It's like an interesting old face, showing a lot of life through it's wrinkles and cracks. And it's a good focal point for all the activity of the harbor. I walk down there all the time. Even in winter I stand and look out where my boat should be moored. It's a very personal formation.

We remember
a painting because it is
powerfully composed.
Any significant piece of work
will be. The viewer may not
be consciously aware of it,
but he remembers. If you
compare a painting to music –
to a song – composition
is a whistleable tune. It is
the harmony of the elements –
size, shape, form, space, line,
color and texture.

10/25/90 20½ X 27½
D'A 300
GHOSTING IN
'CHRISTEEN' OF ESSEX, CN.
LONG ISLAND SOUND LOBSTER
SLOOPS & A SWAMPSOT DORIE

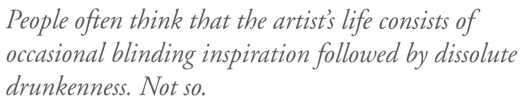

People often think that the artist's life consists of occasional blinding inspiration followed by dissolute drunkenness. Not so.
I find, as most creative people do, that inspiration comes from work.

Art amplifies a longing for harmony, helps make order out of chaos. It's like a sunset, nourishment for the soul.

*Retirement?
How could I retire?
I'd just get up the
next morning and
head out to the studio.
I can't wait to wake up
in the morning
and paint.*

I stood at the famous copse of trees where Pickett's Charge faltered to a standstill in 1863 and tried to imagine myself as one of the aging veterans returning for the 1913 reunion. They numbered over 55,000 – former enemies and their families together on that spot. I was thinking of the incredible power of that physical setting to remind us all of what took place there. I realized that their distance from "their war" was the same as mine from WWII (50 years) and I can no more tell my grandsons what it was really like than they could. And yet, it's worth a try.

*F*rom my studio I can see an old red cedar stump. The stump no longer contains any sharp angles, no bark. The jagged edges left by the saw blade have long since been worn smooth. It has taken on a soft silver patina that emphasizes the bumps and crevices, and it gets more striking as time goes on. I like that. Nature's capacity to gradually return that old stump to the earth. I love wood presented in this way – and individual trees, rather than stylized, generalized ones.

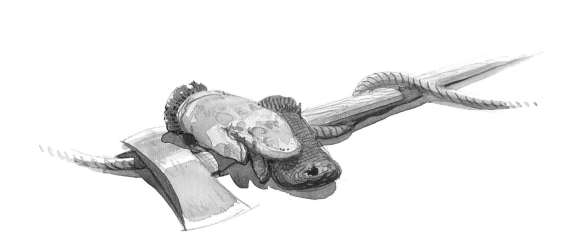

My painting speaks on behalf of the simple pleasures of ordinary life, that having more is not always better.

I don't just paint nostalgia for its own sake. I hope I'm reminding people of values worth keeping – family, work, friendship, community, religious values – of the validity of those things as a way of life.

When I do the pencil sketches as
preliminary work on a new painting, the composition
is a black and white image on the paper, but as I draw
I am visualizing colors and tones. In *RFD*, for example,
I wanted warmth, a pleasant summer day. I wanted to
suggest this place was once fertile, now run down, and
so the colors of the barn, of the day, of the grass, of the
gravel road, all those things are part of my thinking as
I sketch in black and white.

One of my jobs in youth was taking care of horses, which involved some good old fashioned farm work. I'll never forget the exceptional discomfort of chaff inside a sweat-soaked shirt . . . or the immense pleasure of a good cold drink and a swim down in Tyler's Creek.

After a morning rain the road to the mill would be busy . . .

When I saw the mill at Paoli Wisconsin, I instantly imagined my grandfather, maybe as I had depicted him in the earlier painting *Seed Corn*, in that wonderful, golden-hued setting. The architecture of that mill was especially intriguing because the wheel itself is inside – that variation in design, and the fact that mills were the hub of harvesting activity inspired me. It represents the interdependence of farmer, miller and neighbor – and the sense of community that existed in those days.

I remember the church potlucks of my youth – the long tables filled with food and desserts, the steam rising from the dishes. That atmosphere . . . the church and the community that supported it, contains powerful memories for me. In one sense this is an actual place and time, but in another, it is everyone's potluck. I am inviting the viewer to speculate with me. My intent is to evoke the viewer's own rich memories – that's what gives a painting it's special appeal, not my memories, not me.

MAYBE GIRLS GETTING OUT BACK.?

SKY SHADED UPWARD
FROM BLUE VIOLET TO PINK.
LATE SUNLIGHT— PINKS
ON SNOW & SPIRE,

CAST SHADOWS & DARK
WOODS FOR DRAMATIC
CONTRAST.

BRIGHT SKY PINKS IN
REFLECTIONS IN WINDOWS
ON FRONT —— BUT
NO LIGHTS INSIDE.

POTLUCK AT JUDDVILLE (#2)
STANDARD PROPORTION 21 X 28
7/31/91

MOTHER &
2 KIDS —
L.R.

I'm a perfectionist. That gets me into a lot of trouble.

*P*ainting with watercolor is an inexact science. It's like a stain, transparent, and to a degree, not correctable. It bleeds easily on paper, making precision difficult. And the color adheres to minor and otherwise invisible flaws in the paper, exposing them. Excess water can be ruinous. But watercolor is also vivacious, fluid, fresh, exciting . . . it's these magical qualities that challenge me, keep me fascinated.

I love this house. It's in Ephraim. It's old – not much used anymore – with a wooden sunburst up in the gables, and surrounded on three sides by lilacs. It's a simple, ample farmhouse, like so many of that era. And when the family all collected there together, those are remembered as the best of times.

We all owe a great debt to what has gone on before us.

While I often use specific people and places in my paintings, I intend the work to be accessible to people without my peculiar experience. The subjects merely provide me with a language to express the broader message or feeling I am after. If I'm successful, people can experience the same thing that prompted me to paint the scene. Much like a novel, the paintings are based on fact, but I've redigested it.

Like any human, I'm filled with contradictory feelings. Sometimes I feel arrogant, that I can paint as well as any man, immediately followed by the conviction that I can't paint anything at all.

*And there's always the hope that
the next painting
will be closer to perfection.*

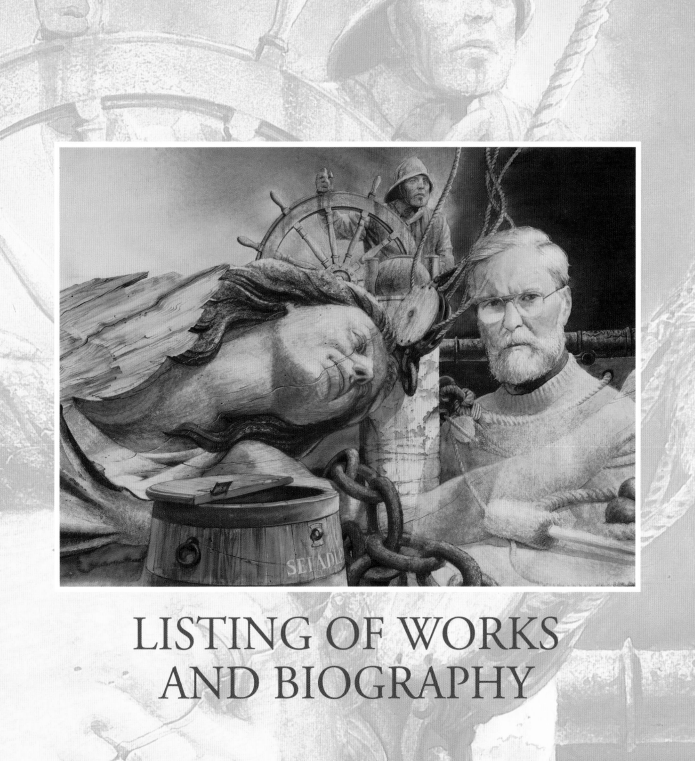

LISTING OF WORKS
AND BIOGRAPHY

All Aboard, 1989
Watercolor, 20 1/2 x 28
Private Collection
Published as a limited edition, 1990
Page 25

Anderson's Store, 1990
Watercolor, 19 1/2 x 28
Private Collection
Published as a limited edition, 1990
Page 26

The Antiquarian, 1988
Watercolor, 21 1/2 x 32 1/2
Private Collection
Page 93

At the Mill, 1992
Watercolor, 20 1/2 x 28
Private Collection
Published as a limited edition, 1992
Page 81

Cant Hook and Logging Chain, 1979
Watercolor, 20 1/2 x 28
Collection of Lorraine and Carl Mengert
Page 71

The Concert, 1990
Watercolor, 21 x 28
The Miller Art Center, Sturgeon Bay, WI
Published as a limited edition, 1990
Page 50

Country Doctor, 1993
Watercolor, 20 1/2 x 28
Private Collection
Published as a limited edition, 1993
Page 90

Early Away, 1990
Watercolor, 17 x 23
The Miller Art Center, Sturgeon Bay, WI
Page 61

Ephraim Winter, 1980
Watercolor, 20 x 28 1/2
Private Collection
Page 23

Evening Lemonade, 1992
Watercolor, 20 1/2 x 29
Private Collection
Published as a limited edition, 1992
Page 72

Evening at the Levee, 1993
Watercolor, 17 1/2 x 28
Private Collection
Published as a limited edition, 1993
Page 63

Family Reunion, 1990
Watercolor, 20 1/2 x 28
Collection of Mr. and Mrs. Keith Hutson
Published as a limited edition, 1991
Page 87

Farmer, 1994
Watercolor, 25 1/2 x 15 1/2
Page 15

First Haircut, 1994
Watercolor, 26 x 20 1/2
Private Collection
Published as a limited edition, 1994
Page 88

Fresh Snow, 1993
Watercolor, 21 x 28
Collection of Mr. and Mrs. Keith Hutson
Published as a limited edition, 1994
Page 33

Harmony, 1994
Watercolor, 20 1/2 x 28
Collection of Mrs. Jacqueline Kellie-Killion,
Published as a limited edition, 1994
Page 84

Haying, 1993
Pencil, 16 1/2 x 25
Jeanine and Ray Jasica Collection
Page 79

John Deere AO 262 101, 1991
Watercolor, 20 1/2 x 28
Private Collection
Published as a limited edition,
Talk Of Spring, 1996
Page 44

Jule Tiden, 1991
Watercolor, 20 x 28
Collection of Mr. and Mrs. Roy Hall
Published as a limited edition, 1992
Page 58

Memory, 1975
Watercolor, 19 1/2 x 27 1/2
Private Collection
Page 40

Morning Fires: Ephraim, 1988
Watercolor, 11 1/2 x 25
Private Collection
Published as a limited edition, 1988
Page 56

Neighbors: A Barn Raising, 1993
Watercolor, 21 x 28
Collection of Mary and David Miller
Published as a limited edition, 1993
Page 48

The Old Becher Place, 1983
Watercolor, 17 1/2 x 23 1/2
Collection of James McMillan
Published as a limited edition, 1983
Page 43

On Valentine Lane, 1992
Watercolor, 20 1/2 x 27
The Miller Art Center, Sturgeon Bay, WI
Published as a limited edition, 1992
Page 64

Potluck at Juddville, 1991
Watercolor, 28 x 21
Collection of Charles Shapiro
Published as a limited edition, 1991
Page 83

Recitation, 1992
Watercolor, 20 1/2 x 28
Collection of Charles R. Koehn
Published as a limited edition, 1992
Page 30

Rendezvous, 1992
Watercolor, 20 1/2 x 28
Collection of Beth and Paul Krueger
Page 38

Return to Gettysburg, 1991
Watercolor, 21 x 28
Friends of the National Parks at Gettysburg
Published as a limited edition, 1991
Page 68

RFD, 1994
Watercolor, 21 x 28
Collection of Suzanne and David Loft
Published as a limited edition, 1994
Page 77

Rounding the Horn, 1991
Watercolor, 28 x 21
Collection of Sue and Jack Anderson
Published as a limited edition, 1992
Page 37

Sabbath at Sea, 1990
Pencil, 21 x 28
Collection of Penny and Al Juozaitis
Page 54

Sabbath at Sea, 1991
Oil on linen, 24 x 36
Private Collection
Published as a limited edition, 1994
Page 55

Seed Corn, 1984
Watercolor, 16 1/2 x 28
Private Collection
Page 80

Sleigh Ride, 1986
Watercolor, 21 x 28
Collection of Carol and Gene McGrevin
Published as a limited edition, 1986
Page 75

The Stall, 1985
Watercolor, 27 1/2 x 21
Collection of Penny and Al Juozaitis
Published as a limited edition, 1985
Page 29

Starting the Day, 1992
Watercolor, 20 1/2 x 28
Collection of Janet and Sherwin Rosenbloom
Page 47

Sunday Hitch, 1989
Watercolor, 21 x 17
Collection of Sara and Bret Tuveson
Published as a limited edition, 1989
Page 28

Swing Your Partner, 1991
Watercolor, 25 1/2 x 20 1/2
Collection of Sarah and William Cowan
Published as a limited edition, 1991
Page 67

Tartar and Pamir, 1990
Watercolor, 20 1/2 x 28
Collection of Carla and Ellsworth Peterson
Page 39

Threshing Floor, 1985
Watercolor, 21 x 28
Collection of Jeanine and Ray Jasica
Page 78

Volunteers, 1993
Watercolor, 21 x 28
The West Bend Mutual Insurance Collection
Published as a limited edition, 1993
Page 35

Wood Sorrell and Mud Bay, 1991
Watercolor, 27 1/2 x 20 1/2
Collection of Eve and Ed Mueller
Published as a limited edition, 1994
Page 52

BIOGRAPHICAL CHRONOLOGY

1927 – Born to Karin E. and Clarence W. Peterson; Elgin, Illinois.

1945 – Graduated from Elgin High School.

1945-46 – World War II service; U.S. Navy, Phillipines to Japan.

1946-51 – Commercial artist; Leo Burnett Advertising Agency and Hart Schaffner & Marx of Chicago.

1949 – American Academy of Art, Chicago; Certificate, Painting and Illustration.

1953 – Marietta College, Ohio; B.A., Art and History.

1954 – Ohio University; M.F.A., Painting and History.

1954-58 – Concord College, West Virginia; Instructor & Assistant Professor of Art and Art History.

1958 – Married Susan A. Gilson, Port Washington, WI.

1959-65 – Three daughters born; Eve, Beth, and Sara.

1959-73 – Marietta College; Associate Professor and Professor of Art, Department Head.

1973-93 – Retired from teaching; Took up residence and full time painting at Ehpraim, Wisconsin.
Free-lance illustrator for *Wooden Boat, Sail,* and *Cruising World* magazines.

1988 – Awarded Honorary Doctor of Humanities by Marietta College.

1989-present – The White Door Publishing Company began national distribution of limited edition prints in "The Memories Collection" and "The Maritime Collection".

1989-present – Mystic Maritime Gallery International Competitions;
Winner of Thomas Hoyne Awards in 1991 and 1992 for paintings best documenting aspects of fishing industry.

1992, 93, 94, 95, 96 – Listed by *U.S. Art* magazine among the 20 best selling artists in the limited edition print industry.